AMAZING ANIMALS OF THE WORLD 1

Volume 9

Spider, Garden — Turtle, Common Musk

GROLIER
an imprint of
SCHOLASTIC
Scholastic Library Publishing
www.scholastic.com/librarypublishing

First published 2008 by Grolier, an imprint of Scholastic Inc.

© 2008 Scholastic Inc.

All rights reserved. Except for use in a review, no part of this book may be reproduced, stored in a retrieval system, or transmitted in any form, or by any means, electronic, mechanical photocopying, recording, or otherwise, without prior permission of Grolier.

For information address the publisher: Grolier, Scholastic Library Publishing
90 Old Sherman Turnpike
Danbury, CT 06816

Printed and bound in the U.S.A.

Library of Congress Cataloging-in-Publication Data
Amazing animals of the world 1.
v. cm.
Contents: v. 1. Aardvark-bobcat — v. 2. Bobolink-cottonmouth — v. 3. Coyote-fish, Siamese fighting — v. 4. Fisher-hummingbird, ruby-throated — v. 5. Hyena, brown-mantis, praying — v. 6. Marmoset, common-owl, great horned — v. 7. Owl, pygmy-robin, American — v. 8. Sailfin, giant-spider, black widow — v. 9. Spider, garden-turtle, common musk — v. 10. Turtle, green sea-zebrafish.
Includes bibliographical references and index.
ISBN 0-7172-6225-1; 978-0-7172-6225-0 (set : alk. Paper) - ISBN 0-7172-6226-X; 978-0-7172-6226-7 (v. 1 : alk. paper) - ISBN 0-7172-6227-8; 978-0-7172-6227-4 (v. 2 : alk. paper) - ISBN 0-7172-6228-6; 978-0-7172-6228-1 (v. 3 : alk. paper) - ISBN 0-7172-6229-4; 978-7172-6229-8 (v. 4 : alk. paper) - ISBN 0-7172-6230-8; 978-7172-6230-4 (v. 5 : alk. paper) - ISBN 0-7172-6231-6; 978-0-7172-6231-1 (v. 6 : alk. paper) - ISBN 0-7172-6232-4; 978-0-7172-6232-8 (v. 7 : alk. paper) - ISBN 0-7172-6233-2; 978-0-7172-6233-5 (v. 8 : alk. paper) - ISBN 0-7172-6234-0; 978-0-7172-6234-2 (v. 9 : alk. paper) - ISBN 0-7172-6235-9; 978-0-7172-6235-9 (v. 10 : alk. paper)
1. Animals—Encyclopedias, Juvenile. I. Grolier Incorporated. II. Title: Amazing animals of the world one.
QL49.A453 2007
590.3—dc22

2007012982

About This Set

Amazing Animals of the World 1 brings you pictures of 400 exciting creatures, and important information about how and where they live.

Each page shows just one species, or individual type, of animal. They all fall into seven main categories, or groups, of animals (classes and phylums scientifically) identified on each page with an icon (picture)—amphibians, arthropods, birds, fish, mammals, other invertebrates, and reptiles. Short explanations of what these group names mean, and other terms used commonly in the set, appear in the Glossary.

Scientists use all kinds of groupings to help them sort out the thousands of types of animals that exist today and once wandered the earth (extinct species). Kingdoms, classes, phylums, genus, and species are among the key words here that are also explained in the Glossary.

Where animals live is important to know as well. Each of the species in this set lives in a particular place in the world, which you can see outlined on the map on each page. And in those places, the animals tend to favor a particular habitat—an environment the animal finds suitable for life—with food, shelter, and safety from predators that might eat it. There they also find ways to coexist with other animals in the area that might eat somewhat different food, use different homes, and so on.

Each of the main habitats is named on the page and given an icon, or picture, to help you envision it. The habitat names are further defined in the Glossary.

As well as being part of groups like species, animals fall into other categories that help us understand their lives or behavior. You will find these categories in the Glossary, where you will learn about carnivores, herbivores, and other types of animals.

And there is more information you might want about an animal—its size, diet, where it lives, and how it carries on its species—the way it creates its young. All these facts and more appear in the data boxes at the top of each page.

Finally, the set is arranged alphabetically by the most common name of the species. That puts most beetles, for example, together in a group so you can compare them easily.

But some animals' names are not so common, and they don't appear near others like them. For instance, the chamois is a kind of goat or antelope. To find animals that are similar—or to locate any species—look in the Index at the end of each book in the set. It lists all animals by their various names (you will find the Giant South American River Turtle under Turtle, Giant South American River, and also under its other name—Arrau). And you will find all birds, fish, and so on gathered under their broader groupings.

Similarly, smaller like groups appear in the Set Index as well—butterflies include swallowtails and blues, for example.

Table of Contents
Volume 9

Glossary

Amphibians—species usually born from eggs in water or wet places, which change (metamorphose) into land animals. Frogs and salamanders are typical. They breathe through their skin mainly and have no scales.

Arctic and Antarctic—icy, cold, dry areas at the ends of the globe that lack trees but are home to small plants that grow in thawed areas (tundra). Penguins and seals are common inhabitants.

Arthropods—animals with segmented bodies, hard outer skin, and jointed legs, such as spiders and crabs.

Birds—born from eggs, these creatures have wings and often can fly. Eagles, pigeons, and penguins are all birds, though penguins cannot fly through the air.

Carnivores—they are animals that eat other animals. Many species do eat each other sometimes, and a few eat dead animals. Lions kill their prey and eat it, while vultures clean up dead bodies of animals.

Cities, Towns, and Farms—places where people live and have built or used the land and share it with many species. Sometimes these animals live in human homes or just nearby.

Class—part, or division, of a phylum.

Deserts—dry, usually warm areas where animals often are more active on cooler nights or near water sources. Owls, scorpions, and jack rabbits are common in American deserts.

Endangered—some animals in this set are marked as endangered because it is possible they will become extinct soon.

Extinct—these species have died out completely for whatever reason.

Family—part of an order.

Fish—water animals (aquatic) that typically are born from eggs and breathe through gills. Trout and eels are fish, though whales and dolphins are not (they are mammals).

Forests and Mountains—places where evergreen (coniferous) and leaf-shedding (deciduous) trees are common, or that rise in elevation to make cool, separate habitats. Rain forests are different (see below).

Freshwater—lakes, rivers, and the like carry fresh water (unlike Oceans and Shores, where the water is salty). Fish and birds abound, as do insects, frogs, and mammals.

Genus—part of a family.

Grasslands—habitats with few trees and light rainfall. Grasslands often lie between forests and deserts, and they are home to birds, coyotes, antelope, and snakes, as well as many other kinds of animals.

Herbivores—these animals eat mainly plants. Typical are hoofed animals (ungulates) that are common on grasslands, such as antelope or deer. Domestic (nonwild) ones are cows and horses.

Hibernators—species that live in harsh areas with very cold winters slow down their functions then become inactive or dormant.

Invertebrates—animals that lack backbones or internal skeletons. Many, such as insects and shrimp, have hard outer coverings. Clams and worms are also invertebrates.

Kingdom—the largest division of species. All living things are classified in one of the five kingdoms: animals, plants, fungi, protists, and monerans.

Mammals—these creatures usually bear live young and feed them on milk from the mother. A few lay eggs (monotremes like the platypus) or nurse young in a pouch (marsupials like opossums and kangaroos).

Migrators—some species spend different seasons in different places, moving to where more food, warmth, or safety can be found. Birds often do this, sometimes over long distances, but other types of animals also move seasonally, including fish and mammals.

Oceans and Shores—seawater is salty, often deep, and huge. In it live many fish, invertebrates, and some mammals, such as whales and dolphins. On the shore, birds and other creatures often gather.

Order—part of a class.

Phylum—part of a kingdom.

Rain forests—here huge trees grow among many other plants helped by the warm, wet environment. Thousands of species of animals also live in these rich habitats.

Reptiles—these species have scales, have lungs to breathe, and lay eggs or give birth to live young. Dinosaurs are thought to have been reptiles, while today the class includes turtles, snakes, lizards, and crocodiles.

Scientific Name—the genus and species name of a creature in Latin. For instance, *Canis lupus* is the wolf. Scientific names avoid the confusion possible with common names in any one language or across languages.

Species—a group of the same type of living thing. Part of an order.

Subspecies—a variety but quite similar part of a species.

Territorial—many animals mark out and defend a patch of ground as their home area. Birds and mammals may call very small or very large spots their territories.

Vertebrates—animals with backbones and skeletons under their skins.

Garden Spider
Araneus diadematus

Length: ¾ inch
Weight: ⅟₆₀ ounce
Diet: flying insects
Method of Reproduction: egg layer

Home: native to Europe; introduced in North America
Order: spiders
Family: orbweavers

 Cities, Towns, and Farms

 Arthropods

© HANS PFLETSCHINGER / PETER ARNOLD, INC

Look outdoors. Can you find a large, round spiderweb? It was likely made by the garden spider. Garden spiders came to North America from Europe long ago.

The garden spider weaves a new web each day. It spins strands of silk from its spinnerets. Spinnerets are special organs near the back of the spider's belly. First, the spider stretches a few strands across the area where it wants to build its web. Next, it stretches a set of strands around the edge. It then threads 25 to 30 strands from the center of the web out to the edge. Finally, it makes long spirals. Now the web looks like a target. Garden spiders can even build webs in outer space. Two garden spiders flew on *Skylab 2* and built perfect webs in orbit.

When its web is complete, the garden spider moves to the center. It waits for an insect or other small animal to become stuck. If an insect flies into a web, the spider will sense the vibration in the strands. It scampers toward the trapped insect and bites it to death. Once the insect has stopped struggling, the garden spider wraps it up in silk. The spider then carries its neat bundle to the center of the web. There it will suck the juicy fluids out of the insect's body. On days when nothing lands in the garden spider's nest, it will eat the web it made the day before. Then it will start work on a new one!

House Spider
Achaearanea tepidariorum

Length: ⅛ to ¼ inch
Diet: insects
Method of Reproduction: egg layer

Home: almost worldwide
Order: spiders
Family: cobweb weavers

 Cities, Towns, and Farms

 Arthropods

© E. R. DEGGINGER / COLOR PIC, INC.

Look in any dark, remote spot in your home. You'll probably find a cobweb. And where there's a cobweb, a house spider is likely nearby. Its web may be a nuisance. But the spider is a helpful creature. It traps and eats insect pests in your home.

House spiders work at night. They build their webs in undisturbed corners. The webs are tangled masses of sticky silk threads. Glands in the spider's belly produce silk as a liquid. This liquid leaves the spider's body through little appendages called spinnerets. As soon as it leaves the body, it hardens to form threads. Because webs catch dust as well as prey, they are called cobwebs. But this annoying "house litter" is actually a death trap. An ant or other prey gets stuck when it touches the threads. When the prey struggles, the motion shakes the web. This tells the spider there is an intruder. The spider hurries over to kill and eat its victim.

The female house spider lays her eggs and bundles them in a silk cocoon. She hangs the cocoon in her web. Newly hatched spiders are not completely developed. They lack mouthparts. But within a few days, they molt to a mature form. Then they leave their mother's web.

Wolf Spider
Lycosa punctulata

Length: about 1 inch
Diet: small insects
Method of Reproduction: egg layer

Home: United States east of the Rocky Mountains
Order: spiders
Family: wolf spiders

Cities, Towns, and Farms

Arthropods

© THEO ALLOFS / ZEFA / CORBIS

Wolf spiders hunt using their keen eyesight to find prey. They have three rows of eyes on their head. The first row has four small eyes. The second and third rows each have two larger eyes. Wolf spiders usually are active at night or when it is cloudy. Their dark color camouflages them among dead leaves, stones, and other ground materials. They spend sunny hours in small burrows dug in soft soil. When wolf spiders hunt, they use methods much like the wolves after which they are named. They do not weave webs. Instead, they chase their prey. They grab a victim with their strong jaws. Then they chew the prey to a pulp and suck up the juices.

Wolf spiders engage in an elaborate courtship dance. The male wolf spider waves the large appendages near his mouth. But after they mate, the male spider must leave quickly—before the female eats him! The female carries the developing eggs in a large egg sac. She attaches the egg to appendages on her abdomen called spinnerets. If the egg sac falls off, the female picks it up and again fastens it to the spinnerets. The young spiders are called spiderlings. After they hatch, they climb up the spinnerets and onto their mother's back. They stay there for about a week, until they are ready to go off on their own. If a spiderling falls off its mother's back, it must quickly climb up the mother's legs. Otherwise, it will be left behind to die.

Arctic Ground Squirrel
Spermophilus parryii

Length of Body: 12 to 16 inches
Length of Tail: 3 to 6 inches
Weight: 1 to 2½ pounds
Diet: seeds, fruits, roots, stems, insects, mice, and leaves

Number of Young: 5 to 10
Home: northern North America
Order: rodents
Family: chipmunks, marmots, and squirrels

 Grasslands

 Mammals

© PAT O'HARA / CORBIS

The Arctic ground squirrel is North America's largest ground squirrel. It hibernates more than half the year. From fall to spring, it escapes the long, cold, dark Arctic winter by snoozing in an underground burrow. When the squirrel awakens, the days are quite long. Throughout June and July, the sun never sets. The Arctic ground squirrel is busy throughout the summer. But it keeps a regular schedule. It forages for food from early morning until late at night. It then returns to its burrow to sleep.

Eating is serious business for the Arctic ground squirrel. From May to August, it must gain enough weight to survive the entire winter. Yet somehow the squirrel still finds time to play. It swims, rolls in the sand, or suns itself.

But the Arctic ground squirrel must constantly watch for hungry predators. Its many enemies include ermines, wolves, Arctic foxes, and grizzly bears. Whenever possible, the squirrel avoids danger by ducking into one of several "escape" burrows. These are short tunnels it has dug a few inches under the ground. However, determined grizzlies often disregard the escape burrows. They simply tear apart the earth to catch the squirrels beneath it.

Eastern Gray Squirrel
Sciurus carolinensis

Length of Body: 8 to 10 inches without tail
Length of Tail: 9 to 10 inches
Weight: up to 1½ pounds
Diet: nuts, fruits, seeds, and insects

Number of Young: 2 to 5
Home: eastern half of the United States
Order: rodents
Family: chipmunks, marmots, and squirrels

 Forests and Mountains

 Mammals

© GARY W. CARTER / CORBIS

The eastern gray squirrel lives in forests in the eastern half of the United States. Many also live in suburban areas and in city parks. With their chattering and chirping, they are noisy little animals.

The gray squirrel is about 18 inches long. Half of its length is its tail! This long, bushy tail serves many purposes. When it rains, it serves as an umbrella. This use is what gave the squirrel its Latin name, *sciurus*. It means "shade tail." It also serves as a blanket during cold weather. If the squirrel falls, it can be used as a parachute. Squirrels are known for making daring leaps from tree branch to tree branch. During leaps, the tail acts to balance the animal.

Squirrels make their homes in trees. They favor oaks, maples, and hickories. Their winter dens are usually in old woodpecker holes. They will also use natural holes in a tree. They do not live in their dens in the summer. Then they build nests of dried leaves and bark where two large branches meet. Squirrels sometimes store acorns, nuts, and other food in their nests. But they usually store food in holes that they dig in the ground. When winter comes, they use their keen sense of smell to locate the nuts.

Squirrels mate during the winter. They give birth in early spring. They usually have two to five offspring. The young stay in the nest for five or six weeks. The squirrels may have a second litter later in the summer.

Red Squirrel
Tamiasciurus hudsonicus

Length: 6½ to 9 inches
Length of Tail: 6 to 8 inches
Weight: 7 to 15 ounces
Diet: seeds, acorns, mushrooms, bird eggs, young birds, and insects

Number of Young: 3 to 7
Home: Canada and northern United States
Order: rodents
Family: chipmunks, marmots, and squirrels

 Forests and Mountains

 Mammals

© RICHARD HAMILTON SMITH / CORBIS

The red squirrel lives in trees throughout much of North America. It has a wide, rust-colored band in the center of its back during the winter. The band grows more olive colored in summer. The belly of the red squirrel is white. It is a tree squirrel and makes great use of its long tail. In strong sunlight the tail shades the animal's back and head. This is the way the squirrel keeps cool. In the rain the tail becomes a natural umbrella. If the squirrel falls from a high place, the tail acts as a parachute. It helps slow the animal's descent. The ears of the red squirrel are larger than those of other tree squirrels. The ears grow hair during the winter.

Throughout the year the red squirrel is active by day. Its scolding-type chatter is a familiar sound in the woods. It is famous for the way it stores its food. It gathers and buries all the essentials during the summer. This gives it a lot of food to eat during the winter months. This creature is a natural environmentalist. Its leftover seeds and acorns take root to form new plants and trees. The red squirrel mates in spring and fall. The female gives birth after 38 days. There are usually three to seven young. They are born in a nest in the hollow of a tree trunk or in a fork in the branches.

The red squirrel lives at least seven years in the wild. It can live up to ten years in captivity. The marten, lynx, and large predatory birds are its principal enemies.

Southern Flying Squirrel
Glaucomys volans

Length: 4 to 6 inches
Weight: 2 to 3 ounces
Diet: nuts, berries, insects, and bird eggs
Number of Young: usually 3 or 4

Home: eastern United States, Mexico, and Guatemala
Order: rodents
Family: chipmunks, marmots, and squirrels

 Forests and Mountains

Mammals

© JOE MCDONALD / CORBIS

Southern flying squirrels do not really fly. They glide through the air. Sometimes they glide for 100 feet or more! Furry membranes of skin join the squirrel's front and back legs. The squirrel jumps and spreads its legs wide. The membranes form a sort of parachute. This enables the squirrel to glide from tree to tree above the forest floor.

Southern flying squirrels prefer old forests where there are plenty of tree stumps and dead trees. They usually make their homes in tree holes and deserted woodpecker nests. Sometimes they will also settle in bird boxes, barns, and attics. Flying squirrels are active only at night. During the day, flying squirrels rest in their homes. They are sociable animals. They often travel from one tree to another in small groups. Their large eyes enable them to see in dim light. Southern flying squirrels feed on many kinds of plants. They also eat insects, young birds, and bird eggs. In fall, they gather nuts, acorns, corn, and other seeds. They store the food in their homes for the winter months when food is scarce.

Newborn flying squirrels are tiny, helpless creatures. They weigh less than 1/5 of an ounce when they are born. They are hairless, and their eyes and ears are closed. The young are completely dependent on their mothers. But they grow quickly. By the time they are five weeks old, they begin to leave the nest. If a baby strays too far, the mother picks it up with her teeth and carries it back to the nest.

Common Starling
Sturnus vulgaris

Length: 7½ to 8½ inches
Wingspan: about 15 inches
Weight: 2 to 3 ounces
Diet: insects and seeds
Number of Eggs: 4 to 7

Home: Eurasia, Africa, New Zealand, Australia and North America
Order: perching birds
Family: starlings

Cities, Towns, and Farms

Birds

© PHILIP MARAZZI; PAPILLO / CORBIS

The starling is native to Europe. It remains one of that continent's most common birds. In 1890, about 80 starlings were imported to the United States. They were brought by a group who wanted to introduce all the birds William Shakespeare mentioned in his plays. The starlings were released in New York City's Central Park. Another 40 starlings were released a year later. The birds multiplied rapidly and spread into surrounding areas.

Today the starling lives in most of North America. Its presence there is a mixed blessing. On the one hand, the starling eats many insect pests, including Japanese beetles, cutworms, and clover weevils. On the other hand, the starling is very aggressive. It competes with native American birds for food and nesting holes.

Starlings live in large flocks, often together with crows, thrushes, and pigeons. During the daytime the birds fly over forests, fields, gardens, and even city dumps in search of food. At the end of the day, the flocks gather together, settle down, and rest. These nighttime resting places are called roosts. Often they contain thousands of birds. Some city roosts in Great Britain contain more than 1 million birds! Starlings make a lot of noise. They chatter continuously, even at night. They have a great variety of calls. Some calls are very musical. Others consist of whistles and squeaks. Starlings also imitate the calls of other birds.

Atlantic Stingray
Dasyatis sabina

Width: up to 2 feet
Diet: mainly mollusks and crustaceans
Method of Reproduction: gives birth to live young

Home: coastal waters from Chesapeake Bay to the Caribbean Islands
Order: stingrays
Family: stingrays, whiprays

 Oceans and Shores

Fish

© JAMES H. ROBINSON / PHOTO RESEARCHERS

The Atlantic stingray is an animal you might want to avoid. Its long tail has poisonous spines. Sometimes a stingray is attacked by a shark or other enemy. Then it whips up its tail and drives its spines into the enemy's body. These barbed spines are hard to pull loose. In the meantime, deep grooves in each spine release poison. Stingray wounds are painful and dangerous. People who swim in stingray habitats need to be careful!

What happens if the stingray loses or breaks a spine? It simply grows a new one. These spines may seem like a perfect way to trap prey. But the ray does not use its tail for this. The Atlantic stingray feeds on clams and other bottom-dwelling animals. It crushes them between its teeth.

The Atlantic stingray lives in warm coastal waters. Sometimes it swims up bays and rivers. These rays have even been caught in the Mississippi River 200 miles upstream! As it swims, the stingray flaps its broad, winglike fins. Usually the stingray lies still in shallow water. Or it is partly buried in silt or sand. Only its eyes are exposed. Its flat, disk-shaped body blends into the surroundings. This makes the animal nearly invisible.

Ocean Sunfish
Mola mola

Length: up to 10 feet
Weight: up to 2 tons
Diet: jellyfish and other invertebrates
Method of Reproduction: egg layer

Home: worldwide in tropical and temperate oceans
Order: cowfishes, filefishes
Family: headfishes, molas

 Oceans and Shores

 Fish

© STEPHEN FRINK / CORBIS

The ocean sunfish gets its name in two ways. It loves to lie in the sun near the surface of the water. And its disk-shaped body looks much like a little sun. But the sunfish goes by many other interesting names. The Spanish call it the moonfish. The English call it the headfish because it looks like it is all head and no body. Still other people call it by its Latin name, *mola*. *Mola* means millstone. Millstones are large, round stones used for grinding grain into flour. This name gives a good idea of the ocean sunfish's size, shape, and weight.

Ocean sunfish have fewer fins than most other fish. They do not have scales. Instead, their skin is protected by a thick, slimy layer of mucus. They are not related to the "sunfish" found in lakes and streams. Their cousins are the pufferfish and other poisonous ocean species. The ocean sunfish, however, is not poisonous. But it is rarely eaten. Instead, people use these fish for the oil in their bodies.

This species is one of the most common fish in the open seas. Though it lives far from the shore in the deep ocean, it usually stays near the water's surface. The sunfish's favorite foods—jellyfish and other invertebrates—are easy for it to catch. So the sunfish spends most of its day drifting lazily on its side. Occasionally it will leap into the air, as if for the fun of it.

Barn Swallow
Hirundo rustica

Length: 6 to 7¾ inches
Diet: insects; occasionally berries
Number of Eggs: 4 to 5
Home: breeds in North America, Europe, and northern Eurasia; winters in South America, sub-Saharan Africa, southern Asia, and Australia
Order: perching birds
Family: swallows

 Cities, Towns, and Farms

 Birds

☐ Summer
☐ Winter

© STEPHEN DALTON / PHOTO RESEARCHERS

This beautiful, delicate bird is a swift and acrobatic flier. Barn swallows dart, twist, and zigzag through the air. They look for flying insects, which they gulp down in their wide, gaping beaks. Barn swallows also swoop over ponds and lakes. They try to catch bugs skimming across the surface. They even drink and bathe on the wing. Then they barely slow down as they dive into the water.

The barn swallow's courtship is a lovely thing to watch. The male pursues his mate-to-be in a long, graceful courtship flight. Eventually the couple land on a roof or tree branch. They lovingly rub each other's head and neck. They even seem to kiss as they gently interlock their bills.

Once they have mated, the couple has serious work to do. It will take the birds one to two weeks to build their nest. They make it out of mud and straw. Originally, this species nested only in caves and cliffs. Today they would rather plaster their nests against the eaves of houses and barns. Sometimes the nests are under bridges and culverts.

The swallow's hatchlings break through their shells just 15 days after the eggs are laid. They fly two weeks after that. This gives the parents time to raise two or three broods in one summer. Often the fledglings from the first clutch of eggs will remain with their parents to help feed the next brood. These older siblings are aptly called "helpers."

Cliff Swallow
Hirundo pyrrhonota

Length: 5 inches
Wingspan: 4¼ inches
Weight: ½ to 1 ounce
Diet: insects
Number of Eggs: 2 to 5

Home: summer, North America; winter, South America
Order: perching birds
Family: swallows

Cities, Towns, and Farms

Birds

☐ Summer
☐ Winter

© DARRELL GULIN / CORBIS

Cliffs and other rocky ledges are not the only places this American swallow builds its nest. It may attach its mud-and-grass nest to the wall of a barn, under the eave of a house, or on the underside of a bridge. Cliff swallows must build their nests carefully because there may be nothing but the stickiness of the mud to keep the nest from falling.

Cliff swallows usually nest in groups. Once they find a good home, they invite all their relatives. A colony may grow to include thousands of mud nests. Sometimes these nests are so close together that they look like a giant cliff swallow apartment building. Scientists believe that cliff swallows live in colonies because it is easier to find food in a group. A cliff swallow that fails to find insects on its own will often return home to the colony. There it waits to see which swallows return with lots of food. It then follows a successful hunter back to where bugs are plentiful.

Life in the colony is far from peaceful. The birds often threaten one another and sometimes battle. What is all the fighting about? Sometimes it is over a mate. Other times it is because one bird has tried to steal mud or grass from its neighbor's nest.

Cliff swallows often try to lay their eggs in a neighboring nest. If one bird can get another to care for its eggs and chicks, then it can lay more in its own nest.

Black Swan
Cygnus atratus

Length: 4 feet
Weight: 9 to 11 pounds
Diet: grasses and grains
Number of Eggs: 4 to 8
Home: Australia and New Zealand

Order: ducks, geese, swans, waterfowl
Family: ducks, geese, and swans

 Freshwater

Birds

© PAM GARDNER / FRANK LANE PICTURE AGENCY / CORBIS

When you think of a swan, you may picture a large, magnificent white bird with a long neck. This is not so in Australia. The swan that lives there is almost all black. It is the only such swan in the world. A species that lives in South America has a black neck and head. The Australian swan, however, has two white areas. One is a ring surrounding its red beak. The other is on the tips of its wings. Its shiny black down is truly beautiful. The black swan can be found on lakes and ponds and in some sea inlets. It eats grass that it pulls from the nearby meadows and weeds from ponds, lakes, and rivers.

In the 1800s, farmers in Australia hunted the black swan for its meat. Its numbers began to decrease. It was hunted during the molting season when the bird is unable to fly. Today the black swan is protected. The black swan was also introduced to New Zealand. It thrives and is a nuisance there. Waterways and flooded meadows do not offer sufficient food. So the swans get much of their food from farmland. Sometimes these birds cause considerable crop damage.

The swan's large, bulky nest is built in the middle of beds of reeds. The female lays four to eight eggs. The young are grayish and become black in their second year. Depending on the region where they breed, black swans may or may not migrate. Like many swans, geese, and ducks, black swans travel at night.

Trumpeter Swan
Cygnus buccinator

Length: 5 feet
Weight: 30 pounds (males); 22 pounds (females)
Diet: herbivore
Number of Eggs: 4 to 6
Home: southern Alaska, western Canada, and northwestern United States

Order: ducks, geese, swans, waterfowl
Family: ducks, geese, and swans

 Freshwater

 Birds

© KENNAN WARD / CORBIS

Before the first Europeans came, there were many trumpeter swans all over North America. Unfortunately, they were hunted for their feathers. They became very rare. By 1932, there were only about 57 trumpeter swans in the United States outside of Alaska. Most of these were bred in Yellowstone National Park. Conservationists set up a reserve of 60 square miles. No hunting was allowed there. By 1954, there were 642 swans. Of those, 370 were bred in the Yellowstone Park reserve. Today, more than 6,000 trumpeter swans live in the United States and Canada.

The trumpeter swan is very similar to the common European mute swan. It has a black beak and an echoing voice. These traits separate it from the European mute swan. The mute swan doesn't make any sounds. The trumpeter swan's name comes from its deep low-pitched cry. It sounds like a trumpet.

In summer, trumpeter swans swim in freshwater lakes and ponds. In winter they move to open water. They can usually be found at river mouths and seacoasts. Trumpeter swans eat mainly water plants and prairie-grass seeds. At nesting time, the female creates a shallow feather-lined pit. It is often built on a pile of water plants. She usually lays four to six eggs. She sits there alone. After 35 days, the chicks hatch. The parents lead them to water. The young grow quickly. By three months of age, they weigh 15 pounds and can fly.

Emperor Tamarin
Saguinus imperator

Length: 7 to 12 inches
Length of Tail: 6 inches
Weight: 9 to 14 ounces
Diet: fruits, plant shoots, insects, eggs, and small vertebrates

Number of Young: 1 or 2
Home: Amazon basin of South America
Order: primates
Family: marmosets, tamarins

 Rain Forests

 Mammals

© LUIZ C. MARIGO / PETER ARNOLD, INC.

The emperor tamarin belongs to a group of small monkeylike animals of the New World. Although they are not classed as monkeys, people often call them monkeys. The emperor tamarin lives in the forests of South America, 3,000 feet above the Amazon River. You can tell the emperor tamarin by its white, drooping mustache, which is over 2 inches long. It got the name *emperor* because of this mustache, which looks like the one worn by Kaiser Wilhelm II, who was a German emperor. The tamarin's round head is silvery brown. Its long thick fur is brownish gray on the shoulders, sides and arms. It is black and white on the throat and chest. Its tail is reddish orange.

The tamarin's fingers have claws instead of nails. Its claws, feet, and long tail help the tamarin move with ease in the trees. There it looks for its food: fruits, plant shoots, insects, eggs, and small animals. Emperor tamarins live in groups of 20 to 30 animals. In captivity, males can be very mean. The hair on their manes sticks up, and they show their sharp teeth to one another. They frequently fight among themselves, often to the death. But in the wild, this behavior is rare.

The mother gives birth to one or two young. In a zoo, a male tamarin was seen helping the mother give birth. He took the newborns, cleaned them, and gave them back to the mother when it was time to nurse.

Brazilian Tapir
Tapirus terrestris

Length of Body: 6 to 7 feet
Length of Tail: 2 to 4 inches
Height: 2½ to 3½ feet
Weight: 400 to 550 pounds
Diet: grasses, aquatic plants, fruits, and buds

Number of Young: 1
Home: South America
Order: odd-toed hoofed mammals
Family: tapirs

  Rain Forests

 Mammals

© TERRY WHITTAKER / CORBIS

? Endangered Animals

From a distance a grazing tapir looks as peaceful as a cow. But it is a mean-tempered creature. Even among themselves, Brazilian tapirs are very quarrelsome. They are quick to fight whenever one trespasses into another's territory. Usually their fights take the form of a dizzying chase. Both animals run in a tight circle, biting at each other's hind legs. Tapirs even bite and chase each other when they mate!

The first European explorer to see a Brazilian tapir thought it was a kind of hippopotamus. Actually, tapirs are more closely related to rhinos and horses. But like hippos, tapirs spend a lot of time up to their nose in water. There they avoid three of their biggest natural problems. These include the burning tropical sun, biting insects, and predators such as jaguars and mountain lions.

Sadly, the Brazilian tapir has not escaped the encroachment of humans. This tapir lives in the rain forests and dry forests of Brazil. In recent years, settlers have slashed and burned both kinds of forest to make way for farms and ranches. In fact, many thousands of acres of Brazilian forest disappear every day. The settlers also shoot great numbers of tapirs for food. The animal is active only at night. But hunters can easily find their prey by using flashlights and headlights. As a result, wherever human villages appear, the Brazilian tapir quickly vanishes. And it is now an endangered species.

Tarantula
Theraphosa blondi

Weight: to 3 ounces
Diet: mostly insects and other spiders; rarely small reptiles, amphibians, and nesting or roosting birds

Number of Eggs: over 100
Home: Central and South America, North America
Order: spiders
Family: tarantulas

 Rain Forests

 Arthropods

© JOHN MITCHELL / PHOTO RESEARCHERS

The largest spiders in the world are known as bird-eating spiders. In North America they are called tarantulas. A tarantula can be 10 inches wide when its legs are spread. You might be afraid of this big, hairy spider. But the tarantula is not dangerous to humans. It rarely attacks, even if provoked. Its bite causes local pain much like a bee sting. Long hair covers its body and its legs. The hairs can irritate human skin.

Tarantulas live in hot regions of the world. You will find tarantulas in the deserts of the American Southwest. They also live in the Amazon forest. Their prickly hair protects them from most predators. The tarantula's only enemy is a hunting wasp. It paralyzes the spider with its sting.

Tarantulas are night hunters. During the day they hide in tree holes or between rocks. At dusk they begin looking for food on the ground or in trees. They pull small mammals, lizards, or hummingbirds from their nests. Tarantulas have fangs, or chelicerae. To kill, tarantulas hold their victims with their legs. They use their fangs to inject poison (venom) into the victim's body. Then they suck out the flesh. The female spider is a hungry meat-eater. She tolerates the male only during the mating season. Even then, he must be very careful not to be eaten by her. The female lays more than 100 eggs. She holds them in an egg case carried by her front legs. The eggs hatch about six weeks later.

Desert Blond Tarantula
Aphonopelma chalcodes

Leg Span: up to 6 inches
Width of Body: about 2 inches
Diet: insects and small reptiles
Number of Eggs: up to 200

Home: Arizona and New Mexico
Order: spiders
Family: tarantulas

 Deserts

 Arthropods

© C. ALLAN MORGAN / PETER ARNOLD, INC.

Tarantulas are the largest spiders in the world. Their venom is deadly only to cold-blooded animals. These include insects, lizards, and snakes. Because they are warm-blooded, humans, birds, and mammals cannot be killed by tarantula venom. In addition to using poison, these hairy spiders also subdue their prey with vicious bites.

Despite the desert blond tarantula's fearsome appearance, many people have been charmed by its calm disposition. When handled gently, it will safely crawl over a person's hands, arms, and body.

The desert blond tarantula has a patch of tiny, irritating hairs on its abdomen. It uses them to discourage predators. When attacked, the tarantula releases these little needles. These act like porcupine quills. Many pet tarantulas have bald spots on their abdomen from the wear and tear of being disturbed too many times.

Tarantulas usually mate during the summer and fall. During mating season, the male desert blond tarantula sets out on a quest across the desert. These bachelor travelers are often seen walking during the late afternoon and evening. When they find a willing female waiting patiently in her burrow, the two mate. The fertilized female desert blond tarantula then lays 100 to 200 eggs in a large silk sac.

Tarpon
Megalops atlanticus

Length: up to 8 feet
Weight: up to 300 pounds
Diet: small fish
Method of Reproduction: egg layer

Home: warm waters off the coasts of the Americas
Order: tarpons
Family: tarpons

 Oceans and Shores

 Fish

© NANCY SEFTON / PHOTO RESEARCHERS

The tarpon is an attractive fish. Its large, silvery scales may be 3 inches across. The tarpon usually lives in tropical waters close to shore. But it may also swim up rivers and into lakes. It frequently breaks the water's surface to gulp in air. It stores the air in an organ called an air bladder. The tarpon has a large mouth. The mouth is filled with rows of small, sharp teeth. These are on the jaws, the roof of the mouth, and the tongue.

A large female tarpon may produce 12 million eggs each year! The eggs hatch at sea into transparent, ribbonlike larvae. The larvae make their way toward shore. They shrink in length at the time they metamorphose (change) into juvenile tarpon.

The young tarpon live and grow in mangrove swamps and other shallow coastal waters. Most of the millions of eggs laid by the female never develop into adult tarpon. Predators eat many eggs, larvae, and juveniles. Pollution of the shallow waters that serve as the tarpon's nursery grounds is also deadly to these fish.

People seldom eat the flesh of tarpon. It is not very tasty. But sports fishermen consider tarpon excellent game fish. When hooked, tarpon fight mightily to escape. They swim to the surface and make spectacular leaps into the air as they try to shake out the hook. Some fishermen who catch tarpon release the fish back into the ocean rather than kill them.

Eastern Subterranean Termite
Reticulitermes flavipes

Length of the Worker: less than ¾ inch
Diet: wood
Method of Reproduction: egg layer

Home: eastern United States and eastern Mexico; introduced elsewhere
Order: termites
Family: subterranean termites

 Cities, Towns, and Farms

 Arthropods

© JAMES ROBINSON / ANIMALS ANIMALS / EARTH SCENES

There are about 1,800 known kinds of termites on Earth. The most common termite in North America is *Reticulitermes flavipes*. It is a major pest because it damages and destroys wooden houses and other wooden structures.

The eastern subterranean termite lives in the ground. When it comes in contact with damp wood, it enters the wood and starts eating. As it eats, it forms tunnels in the wood. It hates light, so the tunnels never open to the surface of the wood. A person looking at the wood cannot tell that it is being destroyed by termites—until the wood collapses.

Wood consists mainly of a material called cellulose. Termites cannot digest cellulose.

Special microorganisms live in the digestive tract of the termites. These microorganisms digest the cellulose so that it can be used by the termites. Without the microorganisms the termites would starve to death.

Termites are social insects that live in colonies. Each colony has a king and queen. The queen has an enormous abdomen and lays eggs for the entire colony. She may lay 3 million or more eggs each year! Most members of the colony are small workers. The workers care for the eggs, feed the queen, collect food, and do other jobs. Soldier termites have huge jaws, which they use to defend the colony against ants and other enemies.

Arctic Tern
Sterna paradisaea

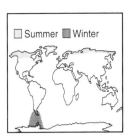

Length: 14 to 17 inches

Diet: fish, crustaceans, worms, and insects

Number of Eggs: usually 2

Home: *Summer:* Arctic Ocean, its islands and coasts;

Winter: area surrounding the southern tip of South America

Order: auks, herons, and relatives

Family: gulls, puffins, terns, and relatives

Oceans and Shores

Birds

Summer ■ Winter

© PAUL VAN GAALEN / ZEFA / CORBIS

The Arctic tern travels long distances. As its name implies, it spends most of the year in the Arctic. But in late autumn, Arctic terns fly some 11,000 miles to Antarctica. By following the sun, the Arctic tern seldom sees the dark of night. In June, July, and August, summer in the northern hemisphere, the North Pole is tilted toward the sun. So the sun never seems to set. In December, January, and February, summer in the southern hemisphere, the South Pole tilts toward the sun. So during that time, it is always daytime in Antarctica.

When it is winter in North America, the Arctic tern fishes in the waters off the southern tip of Chile and Argentina. The bird is at home in the open ocean. So it may be months before it comes ashore.

It returns north in spring. Then the Arctic tern joins others in forming large breeding colonies. This is done on small islands and along the Canadian shoreline. Males and females search for their mates from the previous year. Unmated Arctic terns court each other by running along the beach with their wings raised. Arctic tern couples make simple nests in the sand or on mossy rocks. Sometimes they line the nests with dry grass and bits of shell. The parents take turns warming the eggs. The nest is never unguarded. When the chicks hatch, their parents feed them earthworms and small crabs. The family stays together until they fly to their winter feeding grounds in Antarctica.

Common Tern
Sterna hirundo

Length: 13 to 16 inches
Diet: small fish, crustaceans, and insects
Number of Eggs: 2 to 3
Home: *Summer:* North America and northern Europe;

Winter: south to the tropics
Order: auks, herons, and relatives
Family: gulls, puffins, terns, and relatives

 Oceans and Shores

 Birds

© SIMON MURRAY / PAPILIO / CORBIS

Although this seabird wears a black mask, it is no bandit. Its cousin, the gull, steals whatever food it can. But the common tern works hard and skillfully to catch its dinner. Ninety percent of its diet consists of small fish. The tern catches these by hovering over the water and then rapidly diving with its mouth wide open.

In spring and summer, common terns live in gigantic colonies of tens of thousands of birds. They gather to mate and breed on undisturbed beaches and small islands along the Atlantic coast and on inland lakes. The world's population of common terns was devastated in the 1900s. At that time their tail feathers were popular in ladies' hats. Today the tern is no longer hunted. But its population is still threatened in certain areas. Along the Great Lakes, for instance, aggressive ring-billed gulls are pushing their gentler cousins aside. The gulls also eat the common tern's eggs. In New England many of the tern's nesting sites have been polluted or trampled by humans.

The common tern has a unique way of attacking those who disturb its nest—whether the intruder be gull or human. It flies high over the head of its foe and then swoops. At the lowest point of its dive, the tern lets loose. It hits its enemy with a wet glob of bird droppings. Unfortunately, this well-aimed attack is not always enough to save the tern's eggs from destruction.

Flame Tetra
Hyphessobrycon flammeus

Length: up to 1¾ inches
Diet: small crustaceans, worms, insects, and aquatic plants
Method of Reproduction: egg layer

Home: southeastern Brazil
Order: leporins, piranhas
Family: American characins, characins, and tetras

 Freshwater

 Fish

© BRUNO CAVIGNAUX / BIOS / PETER ARNOLD, INC.

The flame tetra is a tiny but brilliantly colored fish. It lives in the slow-moving freshwater streams and still backwaters of the Brazilian state of Rio de Janeiro. Males and females differ in both color and shape. The fins on the belly of the male are blood red. The female's fins are orange. The female is also heavier and plumper than her mate—especially when she is ready to lay her eggs.

The flame tetra is a timid and peaceful fish. It displays its bright colors only when left undisturbed. Most flame tetras in pet shops are pale in color. This is because the passing customers make them nervous. For its full glory, the tetra must be kept in a clean aquarium with other peaceful fish in a remote corner of the house.

This popular aquarium fish does not need to be harvested from nature. This allows its wild population to thrive. The flame tetra also breeds easily in captivity. To set the stage for romance, the aquarium owner should place a male and female together in their own tank with lots of leafy plants. If the couple is left undisturbed, the male will coax the female to follow him behind the plants. Most couples make about ten trips in and out of their leafy retreat. With each trip the female lays a batch of tiny eggs. But make sure the parents have plenty of tetra food. Otherwise, they will eat their own eggs as soon as they're laid.

Bengal Tiger
Panthera tigris

Length: up to 10 feet
Weight: 400 to 575 pounds
Diet: deer, bovines, pigs, and other animals
Number of Young: 1 to 5

Home: India and Southeast Asia
Order: carnivores
Family: cats

 Forests and Mountains

 Mammals

© FRANS LANTING / CORBIS

? Endangered Animals

The Bengal tiger lives in southern Asia. It was hunted, captured, and poisoned so much that it practically disappeared. It only survived in natural preserves and national parks. It is now strictly protected. Some males occupy a territory of 200 square miles. When there is enough food, the tiger lives in a much smaller territory. It lives in forests, grasslands, or swamps.

The tiger attacks different types of prey. It prefers deer, antelope, pigs, and buffalo. Once in a while, it attacks cattle and even humans. There are many stories about "man-eating" tigers. They're usually old tigers that are sick or wounded and cannot hunt normally. Tigers may also attack humans if their natural environment is destroyed. They will attack humans if their usual prey disappears. As soon as the tiger spots prey, it starts a slow and silent approach. When it is near its prey, it charges. It may jump onto the prey's back. It may pin it down with its powerful claws. It usually kills the prey by biting its throat or neck. The tiger is very strong. It can drag a prey weighing several hundred pounds as much as 1,500 feet to hide the dead animal in bushes or tall grass.

The tiger lives in several lairs. In one of them, the female gives birth to her cubs. When they are eight weeks old, they join their mother on the hunt. At six months, they have learned how to kill. They can feed themselves when they are 16 months old.

Siberian Tiger
Panthera tigris longipilis

Length: up to 13 feet
Weight: up to 650 pounds
Diet: large mammals
Number of Young: 2 to 6

Home: northeastern China, Korea, and eastern Siberia
Order: carnivores
Family: cats

 Forests and Mountains

 Mammals

? Endangered Animals

© JOE MCDONALD / CORBIS

Tigers are the largest of all cats, and the Siberian is the largest tiger. It lives in evergreen forests. The valleys there are where its best hunting and fishing grounds are located. Used to winter weather, this handsome animal has thick, fine fur and a layer of fat that allows it to stand the bitter cold. It moves slowly and silently through the forest, hidden among branches and dead leaves.

The Siberian tiger can eat up to 200 pounds of meat a day. It hunts all kinds of animals: wild pigs, badgers, elk, goats, and sometimes even bears. The tiger is a skilled hunter. It hides and waits for the right moment to attack its victim. With a quick and careful leap, sometimes 23 feet long, it grabs its prey by the throat and slams it to the ground with its powerful paws before killing it.

The mating season for Siberian tigers is in December and January. During this time the males fight over the females. About 100 days after mating occurs, two to six cubs are born.

In 1970, there were only about 130 Siberian tigers left in the world. This huge cat would probably have disappeared, as some other races of tigers have, if actions hadn't been taken to protect it. Since then, the population has grown, although it is difficult to know to what number. Fortunately, many baby Siberian tigers have also been born in captivity—in a number of the world's zoos.

Sumatra Tiger
Panthera tigris sumatrae

Length of Body: 5 to 7 feet
Length of Tail: 2 to 2½ feet
Height at Shoulder: 2½ to 3 feet
Weight: 250 to 500 pounds

Diet: wild cattle and pigs
Number of Young: 2
Home: island of Sumatra
Order: carnivores
Family: cats

Rain Forests

Mammals

Endangered Animals

© LYNN STONE / ANIMALS ANIMALS / EARTH SCENES

Who is the king of beasts? Many would say the tiger, which outweighs even the lion. There are eight varieties of tiger, all of them found in Asia. Two of these subspecies, the Bali and the Javan tigers, may now be extinct. The beautiful Sumatra tiger is in great danger of following them, but there is real hope for its survival. Today, some 200 of these rare tigers survive on the island of Sumatra, many of them in wildlife preserves.

The Sumatra tiger's brilliant orange fur is second in beauty only to that of the Javanese tiger. The Sumatra tiger has more black stripes than do other tigers. Packed closely together, these bold stripes are excellent camouflage in the jungle. The Sumatra tiger also has longer whiskers, which may help the cat feel its way through the darkest part of the forest. Scientists also recognize the Sumatra tiger by its head profile. In other tigers, the forehead juts forward. The Sumatra tiger's forehead is flat and forms a straight line with its muzzle.

Unfortunately for the Sumatra tiger—and all the wildlife of Sumatra—this tropical island has been virtually stripped of trees to make way for coffee, tea, and spice plantations. Wildlife managers have tried to regrow patches of forest. They discovered that once grass takes over a logged jungle, the forest is gone forever. As a result, the Sumatra tiger's habitat is limited to a few large protected areas.

Tufted Titmouse
Parus bicolor

Length: about 5 inches
Weight: less than 1 ounce
Diet: insects, seeds, and
berries

Number of Eggs: at least 5
Home: eastern North America
Order: perching birds
Family: chickadees, titmice

 Forests and Mountains

 Birds

© JOE MCDONALD / CORBIS

The tufted titmouse is part of a large group of birds called "tits." These tiny birds all have short legs and remarkably strong bills, which they use to crack seeds. Tits can be found throughout the world and seldom venture out of the trees and bushes where they feed and make their nests.

The tufted titmouse can be distinguished from the other tits of northeastern America by its spiky crest of head feathers. It was once rather rare. But unlike many other species, the tufted titmouse is actually growing in number. This population boom may be due to the popularity of bird feeders that help the titmice survive the harsh northeastern winter. Tufted titmice prefer to nest in tree holes. If they can't find a naturally occurring hole, they will chip out their own. The female titmouse lines her nest with moss, sometimes throwing in a few feathers and strands of hair. The male spends most of his time defending the territory where his family will live.

Some tits lay as many as 12 eggs at a time. The eggs are white with reddish brown speckles. Ornithologists—scientists who study birds—say that titmice lay so many eggs because their nests are particularly safe places to raise a large family. The parents sit on their eggs for about two weeks before they hatch. It takes another three weeks before the young birds leave the nest.

American Toad
Bufo americanus

Length: 2 to 4 inches
Diet: insects and other small animals
Number of Eggs: 4,000 to 8,000

Home: eastern United States and Canada
Order: frogs and toads
Family: bufonids, toads

 Cities, Towns, and Farms

Amphibians

© LYNDA RICHARDSON / CORBIS

A small American toad sits quietly at the bottom of a plant. It waits and watches with its large eyes. An insect, slug, or other small animal comes near. The toad quickly catches it with its sticky tongue.

American toads liven in gardens and open fields in eastern North America. They are welcome because they eat many pests. In cold weather, they stay underground. They may hibernate if it gets cold enough. When a toad is disturbed, skin glands give off a bad-tasting substance. This keeps predators away.

In the spring, usually during rainy weather, male toads gather together. Their favorite places are ponds, ditches, or other shallow bodies of water. They blow up their throat pouches and sing long, high trills. This attracts female toads. The animals breed in the water. Each female lays her tiny eggs in two long strings The eggs are coated with jelly. And they may weigh several times as much as the mother. The eggs hatch in 3 to 12 days. The young toads, called tadpoles, do not look like the adults. They are small black creatures with gills. They live in water. Their skin gives off poison. This protects them from fish and other predators. The tadpoles gradually change, or metamorphose, into toads that breathe with lungs and live on land.

Western Spadefoot Toad
Spea hammondii

Length: 1½ to 2½ inches
Diet: insects, worms, and crustaceans
Method of Reproduction: egg layer

Home: western United States and Mexico
Order: frogs and toads
Family: North American spadefoots

  Grasslands

Amphibians

© TOM MCHUGH / PHOTO RESEARCHERS

If you were to pick up a western spadefoot toad, you might smell peanuts! When handled, this plump toad produces a slightly poisonous, nutty-smelling slime. The goo can irritate your skin and make your eyes and nose sting and drip.

The western spadefoot's native home is the short-grass prairie of North America. These toads gather in large numbers in sandy areas near shallow water. Many are found on alkali flats and river floodplains. The spadefoot chooses these areas because of their good burrowing soil. Using a hard bump, or "spade," on each hind leg, the toad digs a deep hole. This is its daytime home, the place where the spadefoot stays moist and cool until evening. At night the spadefoot kicks its way out of its burrow, ready to hunt or mate. The male calls for a female while floating lazily on the surface of a pond or other shallow patch of water. His gentle trill sounds like the purr of a cat.

After mating, the female attaches her eggs to underwater plants. The tadpoles hatch in two days and begin gobbling up mosquito larvae. In a month, the tadpoles become small adult frogs, ready to hop onto land.

The western spadefoot shares part of its home with a closely related species, the plains spadefoot, *Scaphiopus bombifrons*. The two species are very similar in size, shape, and color.

Desert Tortoise
Gopherus agassizi

Length: up to 14½ inches
Length of Shell: 12 inches
Weight: 8 to 10 pounds
Diet: grass, occasionally cacti and berries
Number of Eggs: 2 to 14

Home: southwestern United States and northern Mexico
Order: tortoises, turtles, and relatives
Family: tortoises

 Deserts

Reptiles

? Endangered Animals

© THEO ALLOFS / ZEFA / CORBIS

The desert tortoise spends most of the day in its cool, underground burrow. Why does it do this? It cannot survive in the desert's unbearable heat and sun. It emerges only at night or in the early dawn. Then it can be seen slowly walking across the desert sand. It is patiently looking for a bit of tough grass. It is also on the lookout for low-growing berries. There is little juicy vegetation in the desert. So the desert tortoise's body uses moisture very efficiently. The tortoise is also designed to expend as little energy as possible. It sleeps long hours and moves slowly. It even grows slowly. Guess what happens in years when there is little or no rain? The young desert tortoises don't grow at all.

The desert tortoise is sluggish. But in the reptile world, it is smart. Most reptiles wander about with no purpose. The desert tortoise always knows where it's going. It travels far each day for food. But it almost always finds its way back to its own burrow.

Several tortoise species are in danger of extinction. The desert tortoise is one of these. There are many reasons for this. Cars often kill tortoises as they slowly cross desert highways. Farmers and developers have built on the land where the tortoises once lived. Desert tortoises live a very long time. Some may be more than a hundred years old. But we must be more careful if we want them to survive for our grandchildren to see.

Galápagos Tortoise
Geochelone nigra

Length: 4 feet
Weight: 550 pounds
Diet: leaves, fruits, and lichens
Number of Eggs: up to 15
Home: Galápagos Islands off
   Ecuador in the Pacific Ocean

Order: tortoises, turtles, and
   relatives
Family: tortoises

 Forests and
Mountains

 Reptiles

 Endangered
Animals

© STAFFAN WIDSTRAND / CORBIS

The Galápagos Islands are isolated in the Pacific Ocean. They are about 500 miles from the coast of Ecuador. These islands are home to the giant tortoises. The tortoises weigh about 500 pounds each. Galápagos is from the Spanish word for tortoise. In fact there were so many of them on the islands that they were named Galápagos. However, now their numbers are dwindling. Seamen once caught the tortoises. They carried them alive on boats to use as fresh food. Then domestic animals such a dogs, pigs, and goats were brought to the islands. They caused further damage by destroying tortoise eggs. They also destroyed the plants tortoises ate. Forest fires and volcanoes have also killed the tortoises.

Giant tortoises are land animals. They live mainly on lava flows. They need to drink a lot of water. So they travel great distances to reach fresh water located in the mountains. Over the years, paths leading to the mountains have been used by hundreds of tortoises in search of water. They often stay near the water three or four days. They wallow for hours and drink their fill. At night, the temperature drops. The tortoises will remain halfway in the water. Why do they do this? It keeps their body temperature constant. The giant tortoise travels to the coast to lay its eggs. It buries the eggs. They hatch 240 days later. The young run and hide in the tall grass and bushes. They do this because their shells are not hard enough to protect them from the Galápagos hawk. The hawk is the only predatory bird on these islands. The young tortoises creep out in the cool evening hours to get their food.

Toco Toucan
Ramphastos toco

Length: to 26 inches
Diet: mostly fruits, insects, lizards, and the eggs and young of small birds
Number of Eggs: 2 to 4

Home: Central America and tropical South America
Order: woodpeckers, toucans, and relatives
Family: toucans

 Rain Forests

 Birds

© THEO ALLOFS / CORBIS

The toco toucan lives in tropical forests of Central and South America. It is a very big bird, as long as 26 inches. Its body is black with a white throat, neck, and face. The toucan uses its 10-inch orange and black bill to protect its nest and to pluck fruit from trees. The big brightly colored bill helps toco toucans find one another. It's probably used during courtship.

Even with their bright colors, these birds are very hard to see in the forest. They live in treetops, where they are difficult to notice. Therefore, their habits are not well known. They live in groups of about 6 to 12. If they are scared at all, they hide in the hole of a tree trunk. Sometimes they sleep there too. The toco toucans eat small fruits that they swallow whole or bigger ones that

they cut up with their beaks. Generally they take their food with the tip of their beaks and send it with a quick movement of their heads to the bottom of their throats. For dessert, they often eat insects, spiders, or even small birds. Their nests are usually made in holes of decaying tree trunks, lined with fresh leaves. The female lays two to four white eggs that both parents take turns sitting on. At birth, the little toco toucans are blind and have no feathers. They leave the nest after six to seven weeks.

Even though it hides quickly in the forest in the wild, the toco toucan is easily tamed and often kept as a pet. Young toucans are even able to imitate sounds the way parrots do!

Lake Trout
Salvelinus namaycush

Length: 1 to 3 feet
Weight: usually less than 10 pounds
Diet: fish
Method of Reproduction: egg layer

Home: native to northern North America; introduced elsewhere
Order: salmons
Family: trouts and salmons

Freshwater

Fish

© BRUNO MARIELLE / BIOS / PETER ARNOLD, INC.

Until the 1940s, commercial fishers on the Great Lakes caught millions of pounds of lake trout each year. In fact, it was not uncommon to hook a 100-pound lake trout! Such giant specimens are very rare today, even though the lake variety still holds the distinction of being the largest trout of them all. But even a small lake trout makes a very tasty dinner.

So what happened to all those 100-pounders? Through no fault of the lake trout (or people), the Great Lakes were suddenly invaded by a species of sea lamprey. These vicious fish used their suckerlike mouth to attach themselves to—and suck the blood from—the defenseless lake trout. The population of lampreys grew dramatically, while the number of trout fell rapidly. In just a few years, the commercial fishing industry on the Great Lakes was almost wiped out. Fortunately, scientists came to the rescue in the 1960s. They developed a poison that attacks only the lamprey larvae.

The lampreys have been controlled. But the lake trout population has not yet recovered from this disaster. Those that remain still spawn each autumn. The female lays thousands of eggs. Each one takes 16 to 20 weeks to hatch, depending on the water temperature. When newly hatched, lake trout feed on plankton. They begin feeding on fish as they get bigger.

Rainbow Trout
Oncorhynchus mykiss

Length: up to 28 inches
Weight: up to 15 pounds
Diet: insects and fish
Method of Reproduction: egg layer

Home: native to Canada and the United States
Order: salmons
Family: trouts and salmons

 Freshwater

 Fish

© DALE C. SPARTAS / CORBIS

Rainbow trout are among the most familiar game fishes in North America. They are widely caught and eaten. In addition to wild specimens, rainbow trout are bred on fish farms and then released into the wild. Rainbow trout are named for their colorful bodies. The back is greenish, the belly is silvery, and there is a reddish strip running along each side of the body. Many small black spots dot the head, body, and fins.

Most rainbow trout live in cold rivers and lakes that contain a rich supply of oxygen. One variety, however, migrates to the sea when it is about two years old. It returns to rivers only to breed. This variety, called steelhead trout, is colored in shades of silver and blue.

In late winter and early spring, the female scoops out a nest in gravel at the bottom of a river and lays her eggs, which the male then fertilizes. The female covers the eggs with gravel or sand, to hide them from predators. After the eggs hatch, the young fish—called fry—remain in the gravel for a while. During this time, food comes from a yolk sac that is attached to the belly. When the yolk has been consumed, the fry begin to move into open water to feed on microscopic plants and animals. As they get bigger, they are able to catch water-borne insects. Only large adults feed regularly on fish.

Bluefin Tuna
Thunnus thynnus

Length: up to 16 feet
Weight: up to 900 pounds
(record: 1,800 pounds)
Diet: fish, squid, and large crustaceans
Number of Eggs: up to 1 million

Home: worldwide in tropical and temperate oceans
Order: perch-like fishes
Family: albacores, bonitos

 Oceans and Shores

 Fish

© JEAN-PIERRE SYLVESTRE / PETER ARNOLD, INC.

The bluefin tuna is the largest of all species of tuna. It is also a very important food fish for people in many parts of the world. It can grow to a length of 16 feet and a weight of 1,800 pounds. But almost all bluefins are captured long before they become giants. Most of the bluefins caught by fishermen off the Pacific coast of North America weigh between 10 and 45 pounds.

Bluefins have sleek, streamlined bodies. Their tough skin is covered with tiny scales. These allow the creature to glide easily through water. Bluefins have been clocked at speeds of more than 40 miles per hour. They can also leap out of the water, giving fishermen a real challenge. These fish travel in groups called schools. Some people call these fish "wolves of the sea" because they chase their prey like packs of wolves. Bluefins feed mainly on small fish that swim in large groups, such as herring, mackerel, and flying fish. The main enemy of the bluefins is the killer whale.

Bluefins do not live in the same area year-round. In spring, bluefins migrate thousands of miles to their spawning grounds in cool waters. Later in the year, they return to their feeding grounds in warmer waters. A female may lay 1 million or more eggs that hatch within two days. A newborn tuna is less than ⅕ inch long, but it grows rapidly. By the time a bluefin is a year old, it is 2 feet long and weighs as much as 11 pounds.

Turkey
Meleagris gallopavo

Length: 4 feet (male); 3 feet (female)
Weight: 16 pounds (male); 9½ pounds (female)
Diet: seeds, nuts, fruits, grains, insects, and small vertebrates

Number of Eggs: 8 to 15
Home: eastern and central North America
Order: pheasants, quails, and relatives
Family: grouse, partridges

 Forests and Mountains

 Birds

© JOE MCDONALD / CORBIS

Many years ago, Benjamin Franklin nominated the turkey to be the U.S. national bird. It lost out to the bald eagle. But the turkey still holds a special place in American tradition.

The turkey is common in North America—its original home. It was introduced in Europe in the 1500s by the Spaniards. Later, the English brought the domesticated turkeys back to North America. There were many wild turkeys in the forests from southern Canada all the way to Mexico. Many were killed by hunters. But their population has increased dramatically in recent years.

The wild turkey is thinner than its domestic relative. It has tan feathers. They are dotted with beautiful sparkling green flashes. The wild turkey has a hairless bluish head. It is adorned with fleshy growths and brightly colored hanging folds.

Wild turkeys live in small groups in the forest. They feed on seeds and insects. They will also eat fallen fruit. Their sense of sight is highly developed. They notice the smallest motion anywhere near them. Male turkeys fight fiercely during the mating season. Sometimes they fight to the death. The winner shows off his tail. Then he sticks out his chest. Finally, he gives off a loud gobble to attract females. The female turkey lays her eggs in a nest built on the ground. She covers the eggs with leaves and grasses when she goes away.

Lantham's Brush Turkey
Alectura lathami

Length: 23 to 27 inches
Diet: seeds, fallen fruits, and insects
Number of Eggs: 12 to 16

Home: eastern Australia
Order: pheasants, quails, and relatives
Family: mound-building birds

 Rain Forests

 Birds

© ERIC AND DAVID HOSKING / CORBIS

Latham's brush turkey grunts and clucks as it walks through the thick forests of eastern Australia. The turkey spends most of its time looking out for anything that could possibly spell trouble. When it is frightened, it runs to the nearest shrub or escapes up a tree.

The turkey's most distinctive feature is its red, featherless head. The head and neck are small compared with its long, stout body. Latham's brush turkey has a bright ring of yellow skin around the lower part of its neck.

The male is the nest builder in the family. He forms a huge mound of soil, leaves, and other plant matter gathered from the forest floor. The nest may be 6 feet high and 12

feet wide! There the female lays her eggs, one at a time over the course of a few days. She places each egg in a different part of the mound. The eggs are incubated, or warmed, by heat given off by decaying plants in the nest. The male controls the temperature of the nest by using his bill like a shovel. He creates air passages in parts of the mound that are too warm. He adds decaying plants to the cooler sections.

In about seven weeks the baby turkeys peck their way out of the eggshells. Then they must dig an escape route through the huge mound of rotting plant matter. When they reach the outside, they are on their own.

Common Box Turtle
Terrapene carolina

Length: up to 6 inches
Diet: berries, fruits, snails, and worms
Number of Eggs: 2 to 7
Home: eastern half of the United States

Order: tortoises, turtles, and relatives
Family: box turtles and pond turtles

 Freshwater

 Reptiles

© DAVID A. NORTHCOTT / CORBIS

The common box turtle can live for more than 100 years. It probably lives longer than any other kind of animal in the United States. One thing that helps it survive so long is its special suit of armor. The common box turtle and the western box turtle are close relatives. They are the only turtles that can close themselves up tightly and completely in their shells. When attacked or threatened, the turtle pulls its head and four legs inside the shell. There are special hinges at the front and back of the shell. These are located where the top and bottom parts meet. They lock in place. Then the turtle is snug and safe in its box. Box turtles have to be careful not to eat too much. If they get too fat, their shells won't close completely.

The common box turtle is found in the eastern half of the United States. It lives in wooded areas. Its home is usually near streams and in other damp places. It does not like hot and dry weather. Then it will burrow into the mud. Just its head will stick out.

Eggs are laid during late spring and early summer. They do not hatch until fall or winter. The young sometimes spend the winter in the nest. Young box turtles eat worms and caterpillars. They also eat snails. But adult box turtles eat mostly berries and fruit. They will also eat leaves. In captivity, they eat meat, lettuce, and other greens. They will even eat bananas and bread. They are gentle creatures and make excellent pets.

Common Mud Turtle
Kinosternon subrubrum

Length: 3 to 5 inches
Diet: worms and other invertebrates
Number of Eggs: 1 to 6
Home: eastern United States

Order: tortoises, turtles, and relatives
Family: mud turtles, musk turtles

 Freshwater

 Reptiles

© DOUG WECHSLER / ANIMALS ANIMALS / EARTH SCENES

In summer, common mud turtles can often be seen prowling along the bottom of shallow ponds and slow-moving streams. These little turtles hunt for worms and other small creatures that they dig from the mud. During times of drought, the mud turtle's home may dry up completely. When this happens, some mud turtles burrow into the ground and wait for rain. Others walk through nearby forests looking for new ponds and streams. Unfortunately, the mud turtle's journey may take it across rural roads. As a result, many of these creatures are accidentally run over by passing cars.

Some mud turtles allow themselves to be handled. But not all individuals are so tolerant. Many do not hesitate to bite.

People and pets have another reason to avoid the mud turtle. Like other members of its family, this turtle has two pairs of glands just beneath the edge of its shell. The musk from these glands stinks!

Mud turtles take five to seven years to mature into adults, ready to mate. After breeding in early spring, the female lays her eggs in June. She digs a small hole in wet sand or rotten weeds. There she deposits several brittle pinkish or bluish white eggs. Some mud turtles leave their inch-long eggs in abandoned muskrat or beaver lodges, which they must enter from beneath the water. In Florida, older females continue laying eggs year-round.

Common Musk Turtle
Sternotherus odoratus

Length: 3 to 6 inches
Diet: insects, algae, and carrion
Number of Eggs: 2 to 9
Home: eastern North America

Order: tortoises, turtles, and relatives
Family: mud turtles, musk turtles

Freshwater

Reptiles

© JAMES R. FISHER / PHOTO RESEARCHERS

Have you ever been tempted to catch a turtle for a pet? If so, stay away from the common musk turtle. This cute little creature looks harmless. But in nature, looks are often deceptive. Common musk turtles hate to be handled. If you try to pick one up, it will claw and bite—hard! Then it will unleash its secret weapon, and you'll know how this species got its nickname, the "stinkpot" turtle. Few people will ever bother this turtle twice!

This common musk turtle's foul odor comes from musk glands on either side of its body. They are located just beneath its shell. The turtle's musk is more than a weapon. Like many animals, it uses its strong scent to communicate with others of its kind. A male musk turtle who wants to mate will approach a female and begin to

nudge her. If she likes the affection, she lets him know. She raises a stink—from her musk glands, that is.

Common musk turtles mate and build their nests on land. They spend the rest of their lives almost entirely in water. They can be found in ponds, streams, and canals. Sometimes, the musk turtle will float just below the surface. It holds its nostrils above water for a breath of fresh air. In this way the turtle can also soak up the warmth of the sun while lazily looking for the occasional insect meal to buzz by. Musk turtles must be careful to escape predators. Despite their smell, they are a favorite snack for herons, raccoons, and crows. A musk turtle that can avoid life's dangers, however, can live to a ripe old age of 50.

+ R
590.3 A
v. 9

Friends of the
Houston Public Library

Amazing animals of the world
1.
Montrose JUV REF
05/08